WHO DID YOU REALLY MARRY?

Love Languages, Personality Types, Communication

PARTICIPANT'S GUIDE

FOCUS
THE FAMILY

TYNDALE HOUSE PUBLISHERS, INC.
Carol Stream, Illinois

CONTENTS

QUICK START GUIDE FOR COUPLES

Whether you're studying in a group, as a couple, or individually, this book is for you. It's packed with discussion questions, advice, biblical input, and application activities.

But maybe all you'd like to do right now is watch the accompanying DVD and talk about it with your spouse. If so, go directly to the "Catching the Vision" section of each chapter. There you'll find the discussion questions you're looking for.

When you have more time, we encourage you to explore the other features in this book. We think you'll find them . . . essential!

For even more help with your relationship, go to
focusonthefamily.com/marriage.

WELCOME!

If there's anything you don't need, it's one more thing to do.

Unless, of course, that one thing might make the *other* things a whole lot easier.

We can't guarantee that this course will take all the challenge out of your marriage. It won't keep you from forgetting your anniversary, thaw all the icy silences, or make your spouse alphabetize the shoes in your closet.

But it *will* help you understand why you're married, how to stay that way, and how to enjoy it to the fullest. That's because you'll learn the essentials—what's vital to a healthy relationship, keys to working out your differences, and what God considers most important in "holy matrimony."

In other words, you'll discover how to be the husband or wife you really want to be.

That takes effort, but it doesn't take boredom or busy work. So we've designed this course to be provocative and practical. At its heart is an entertaining, down-to-earth video series featuring many of today's most popular marriage experts. And in your hands is the book that's going to make it all personal for you—the Participant's Guide.

In each chapter of this book, you'll find the following sections:

Finding Yourself. Take this survey to figure out where you stand on the subject at hand.

Catching the Vision. Use this section as you watch and think about the DVD.

Digging Deeper. This Bible study includes Scripture passages and thought-provoking questions.

Making It Work. Practice makes perfect, so here's your chance to begin applying principles from the DVD to your own marriage.

Bringing It Home. To wrap up, a licensed counselor affiliated with Focus on the Family offers encouraging advice you can use this week.

Whether you're using this book as part of a group or on your own, taking a few minutes to read and complete each chapter will bring the messages of the DVD home.

And isn't that exactly where you and your spouse need it most?

Note: Many issues addressed in this series are difficult ones. Some couples may need to address them in greater detail and depth. The DVD presentations and this guide are intended as general advice only, and not to replace clinical counseling, medical treatment, legal counsel, or financial guidance.

Focus on the Family maintains a referral network of Christian counselors. For information, call 1-800-A-FAMILY and ask for the counseling department. You can also download free, printable brochures offering help for couples at http://www.focusonthefamily.com/marriage/articles/brochures.aspx.

Chapter 1

OPPOSITES ATTRACT

"When she's stressed out, she talks all the time. If I get tired of talking to her after an hour or so, she gets a second wind and calls a friend!"

"He's so sensitive. I can't correct him without it making him angry. No matter what I say, he takes it wrong."

"After we leave a social event, I get so angry I can't see straight. She embarrasses me—not once, but throughout the evening."

If these statements hit home, you're not alone. Most of us have said—or at least thought—similar things about our spouses.

Couples often tell therapists that one of their toughest challenges is adjusting to a spouse's personality. Many of those people are ready to give up and resign themselves to a miserable state of existence. Others fear their situations will worsen to a point where the spouse's personality turns repulsive—and divorce will be inevitable.

So what do you do? Stay miserable? Get angry and resentful? Leave?

We suggest none of the above.

—Mitch Temple
Licensed Marriage and Family Therapist[1]

FINDING YOURSELF

Identifying Your Needs

This survey will help you think about how you're already handling the issues discussed in this session.

1. If you and your spouse were musical instruments, what kind would you be? Why?
   ___ handbells in a choir
   ___ dueling banjos
   ___ an electric guitar and an acoustic guitar
   ___ a gloomy oboe and a perky flute
   ___ a loud trombone and a muted trumpet
   ___ other _____

2. When it comes to marriage, which of the following sayings do you agree with? Why?
   ___ "Opposites attract."
   ___ "It takes all kinds."
   ___ "Birds of a feather flock together."
   ___ "It takes one to know one."
   ___ "Men are from Mars, women are from Venus."

3. Which of the following ideas do you think are false? Why?
   ___ God has one person picked out for you.
   ___ You need to find your soul mate.
   ___ Some personality types are incompatible.
   ___ It's a good idea to understand your spouse's personality type.
   ___ Generally speaking, gender determines personality type.
   ___ If you married the "wrong" type, you'll be miserable.

4. Did you and your spouse take a personality test before marriage? If not, why not? If so, what effect did it have? _____

_____

5. Would you say that your parents were the right "type" for each other? Why or why not? _____

_____

6. What does it mean to say that spouses are "perfect for each other"? Does this describe any couples you know? _____

_____

CATCHING THE VISION

Watching and Discussing the DVD

"It takes all kinds." But when two very different kinds find themselves in the same marriage, the results aren't always pretty. Often the contrasts that attracted couples end up repelling them.

In this DVD segment, bestselling author and counselor Dr. John Trent looks at the differences between spouses—and how concentrating on strengths can make those differences assets instead of liabilities. Host and counselor Dr. Greg Smalley adds a story from his own family, too.

You'll have fun deciding what types you and your spouse are, and how to make the most of it.

After viewing the DVD, use questions like these to help you think through what you saw and heard.

1. What do spouses usually mean when they say the following? Do you think these sayings are facts, half-truths, romantic notions, or myths? Why?

- "Opposites attract."
- "You complete me."
- "She's my better half."
- "He's everything I'm not."
- "I don't know what I'd do without her."

2. According to Dr. John Trent, what are the four personality types? If you were to express them not as animals but as different kinds of cars, what would they be?

3. Which of the following "personality pairs" do you think would get along better? Why?
   - lion and lion
   - lion and golden retriever
   - otter and otter
   - otter and beaver

4. Let's say a couple has to decide whether to move 1,000 miles away so that the husband can take a new job with more pay and bigger challenges. All the wife's friends are in the current location, and neither spouse knows anyone in the new place. How might each of the following personality combinations approach the question, and what do you think each couple would decide? Why?
   - otter wife and beaver husband
   - lion husband and golden retriever wife
   - two golden retrievers
   - two otters

5. John Trent points out that lions tend to approach problems aggressively; golden retrievers tend to step away from problems. How could spouses with these personalities serve as "checks and balances" on each other in the following situations?

- The couple's 12-year-old son is on a soccer team, but the coach hardly ever lets him play.
- The couple's 10-year-old daughter won't practice her piano playing between lessons.
- The couple's 14-year-old cat will die without a $7,500 operation.
- The "golden retriever's" widowed 80-year-old mother is no longer able to take care of herself.

6. How would you describe your personality type and that of your spouse? What conflicts do you think John Trent would expect you to have? Do you actually tend to have them? If not, why not?

7. How have personality differences between you and your spouse played a positive role in your marriage? If your spouse suddenly swapped personalities with someone else, what would you miss most about those differences?

Bible Study

As Jesus and his disciples were on their way, he came to a village where a woman named Martha opened her home to him. She had a sister called Mary, who sat at the Lord's feet listening to what he said. But Martha was distracted by all the preparations that had to be made. She came to him and asked, "Lord, don't you care that my sister has left me to do the work by myself? Tell her to help me!"

"Martha, Martha," the Lord answered, "you are worried and upset about many things, but only one thing is needed. Mary has chosen what is better, and it will not be taken away from her." (Luke 10:38-42)

1. Are you more like Mary or Martha? Is your spouse more like Martha or Mary? If the two of you have differences in this area, has it caused conflict?

2. Did Jesus imply that Mary's personality was superior, or that she'd made a better choice? How can a spouse's choices make a bigger difference than personality type?

> When the time came for [Rebekah] to give birth, there were twin boys in her womb. The first to come out was red, and his whole body was like a hairy garment; so they named him Esau. After this, his brother came out, with his hand grasping Esau's heel; so he was named Jacob. Isaac was sixty years old when Rebekah gave birth to them.
>
> The boys grew up, and Esau became a skillful hunter, a man of the open country, while Jacob was a quiet man, staying among the tents. Isaac, who had a taste for wild game, loved Esau, but Rebekah loved Jacob.
>
> Once when Jacob was cooking some stew, Esau came in from the open country, famished. He said to Jacob, "Quick, let me have some of that red stew! I'm famished!" (That is why he was also called Edom.)
>
> Jacob replied, "First sell me your birthright."
>
> "Look, I am about to die," Esau said. "What good is the birthright to me?"
>
> But Jacob said, "Swear to me first." So he swore an oath to him, selling his birthright to Jacob.
>
> Then Jacob gave Esau some bread and some lentil stew. He ate and drank, and then got up and left.
>
> So Esau despised his birthright. (Genesis 25:24-34)

3. How would you describe the personalities of Jacob and Esau? How might spouses with those personalities interact?

4. Isaac and Rebekah each preferred one son over the other. What happens when spouses prefer their own personalities and wish their mates were more like themselves?

> *Now you are the body of Christ, and each one of you is a part of it. And in the church God has appointed first of all apostles, second prophets, third teachers, then workers of miracles, also those having gifts of healing, those able to help others, those with gifts of administration, and those speaking in different kinds of tongues. Are all apostles? Are all prophets? Are all teachers? Do all work miracles? Do all have gifts of healing? Do all speak in tongues? Do all interpret? But eagerly desire the greater gifts.*
>
> *And now I will show you the most excellent way.*
>
> *If I speak in the tongues of men and of angels, but have not love, I am only a resounding gong or a clanging cymbal. If I have the gift of prophecy and can fathom all mysteries and all knowledge, and if I have a faith that can move mountains, but have not love, I am nothing. If I give all I possess to the poor and surrender my body to the flames, but have not love, I gain nothing.*
>
> *Love is patient, love is kind. It does not envy, it does not boast, it is not proud. It is not rude, it is not self-seeking, it is not easily angered, it keeps no record of wrongs. Love does not delight in evil but rejoices with the truth. It always protects, always trusts, always hopes, always perseveres.*
>
> *Love never fails. But where there are prophecies, they will cease; where there are tongues, they will be stilled; where there is knowledge, it will pass away. For we know in part and we prophesy in part, but when perfection comes, the imperfect disappears. (1 Corinthians 12:27–13:10)*

5. According to this passage, how can people with different strengths work together?

6. Do you believe that love can overcome personality differences in a marriage? Why or why not?

MAKING IT WORK

Applying the Principles

John Trent says that understanding our strengths helps us see why our spouse is so valuable; that helps us blend differences and become a close-knit team.

To help you start thinking about your strengths and how they might complement each other, here's a fun exercise. Try seeing yourself and your spouse as superheroes. What would your "powers" be? List them here.

What would your names be? (Examples: Intuitive Girl; The Human Calculator)

What would your costumes look like? Draw them on the figures below.

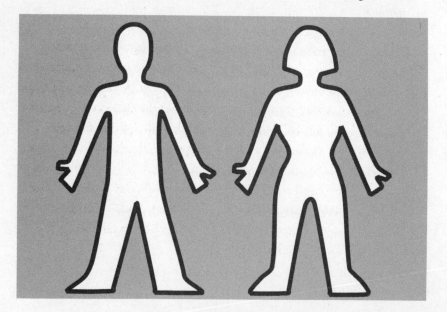

How could your powers complement each other as you faced a threat? Let's say the two of you face a supervillain called The Budget Buster. How could you work as a team to overcome him? Draw your idea in the "comic strip" below.

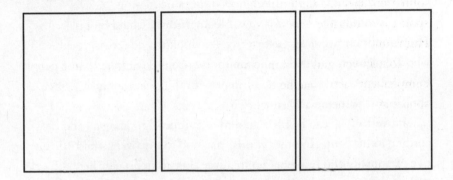

How could seeing yourselves as this kind of team affect the way you get along? How could you use that kind of cooperation and finding strength in differences to overcome challenges you're currently facing?

Here are two ways you can continue to follow up on this session. This week, rent a movie featuring a man and woman with very different personalities. Some possibilities: *Romancing the Stone, The King and I,* and *The Music Man.* Spend some time talking about the characters' contrasts, conflicts, and "chemistry." How do you think a relationship between them would have worked out over the long term? How could your own differences be part of the "adventure" of marriage?

If you'd like to find out more about your personality types, see *The Two Sides of Love* by Gary Smalley and John Trent, Ph.D. (Tyndale, 1990). To take a test from that book, go to http://listen.family.org/images/PersonalStrengthsSurvey.pdf.

BRINGING IT HOME

Encouragement from a Counselor

Consider these facts about differences in personalities.

1. *God created us to be different.* He knew there would be a place in His plan for introverts and extroverts, for thinkers and feelers, for those who are planners and those who are spontaneous. He created some people to be dreamers and some to be content with things as they are. "Different" doesn't automatically equal "wrong."

Proverbs 22:6 can be translated to recommend training a child "according to his bent." In other words, it's good to discover a child's distinctive personality and bring her up in a way that compliments her personality instead of tearing it down. Why not apply this idea to marriages, too? Are you willing to allow your spouse the same freedom to be unique—and not the same as you?

2. *It's easier to spot a flaw than to see a strength.* Jesus put it in terms of spying a speck in another's eye versus seeing a log in our own (Matthew 7:3-5).

When you were dating, you probably found it easy to focus on the admirable traits of your future mate. You seemed to like the same things, enjoyed the same conversational topics, and tended to overlook each other's quirks.

Bennett, for instance, married Deb because she was such a "great communicator." Now he's annoyed because she's such a "great agitator." Dana married Marcus because he was such a "confident, strong manager." Now he's an "overconfident jerk."

3. *Your ability to tolerate your mate's personality changes with time.* Most of us can stand negative behavior for a while. But everyone has a limit!

Belinda, for example, could put up with Jeff's ability to make a joke out of everything—for about a year. After she became the brunt of his jokes, her level of tolerance changed. She reached a point where she despised his voice, especially his laughter.

Is that the case with you? Maybe it's not that your spouse's personality has become more of a problem; it may be that your ability to value or overlook some attributes has diminished.

Reaching your limit is no excuse for giving up on a marriage, though. Sometimes it's enough to realize that the change is in your "irritation threshold" and adjust that gauge accordingly. At other times, you may need help from a counselor to express your frustration and find a healthy tolerance level.

4. *Sometimes it's not really about personality.* Could it be that your mate has done something that deeply hurt you—and his personality has become the contention point?

That was the case with Barry. He'd always liked the fact that his wife, Wendy, was sociable and outgoing. But then he discovered that she'd been flirting with a coworker. Now Barry viewed her personality as a threat.

When your spouse hurts you, it tends to change the way you think and feel toward him or her. You suddenly see that person through tinted lenses, not clear ones.

If this is the case with you, healing has to occur before everyday personality issues can be objectively dealt with. Identify the real issue. Work on it—with the help of a counselor if needed. Commit to overcoming your tendency to focus on the negative aspects of your spouse's personality.

Your mate's personality may be different and sometimes difficult to manage. But God doesn't want this to allow division in your marriage.

One of Paul's points to the Corinthians might be summarized this way: "Learn to accept and adjust to each other, no matter what people look like or act like." That applies to husbands and wives, too.

—Mitch Temple
Licensed Marriage and Family Therapist[2]

Chapter 2

LET'S TALK (PART 1)

Caleb and Trina, recently married, didn't have much spare time. They had full-time jobs and took evening classes. Already active in their church, they were approached one day by a church leader who said there was a desperate need for a young couple to lead the junior high group.

They didn't say no. How could they? After all, they'd been married in that church. And they were interested in doing "full-time" ministry someday.

After months of hard work, they found themselves overinvested in church work and underinvested in each other. They spent little time together, and found even less time to converse. When they did talk, it was mostly to argue and criticize each other.

One day, Caleb went to a car lot and looked at the hundreds of sleek, clean vehicles. After some wistful daydreaming, he got back in his own sedan.

It was a glorious afternoon for a drive in the country, so he drove—and kept driving. Long into the evening, about two miles from home, the car suddenly stopped. It had run out of gas.

Something came to Caleb's mind at that moment: His marriage was running out of fuel, too. He thought about how much he'd enjoyed the afternoon drive without his wife. This was an ominous sign, he knew.

Like Caleb and Trina, many couples don't take enough time to talk, bond, and firmly connect with each other. But it doesn't have to be that way.

—James Groesbeck
Licensed Marriage and Family Therapist[3]
with Amy Swierczek

FINDING YOURSELF

Identifying Your Needs

Take a couple of minutes to fill out the following survey.

1. Which of the following phrases best describes your communication style as a husband or wife? What might your spouse think of your answer?
   ___ *The Sounds of Silence*
   ___ "Speak softly and carry a big stick."
   ___ the Great Communicator
   ___ "Shout, shout, let it all out."
   ___ "Let me hear your body talk."
   ___ other _____

2. Which of the following is most like your spouse's communication style? Why?
   ___ text messaging
   ___ video conferencing
   ___ hieroglyphics
   ___ e-mail
   ___ opera
   ___ other _____

3. What percentage of the communication time in your marriage would you guess is spent on each of the following? How do you feel about that?
   ___ forgiving
   ___ complaining
   ___ celebrating
   ___ blaming

_____ encouraging

_____ apologizing

4. Do you think spouses in Bible times were as concerned about communication as they are today? Do you think they should have been? Why or why not? _____

_____

5. What was the last time you really enjoyed communicating with your spouse? _____

_____

6. What's the next time you expect that to happen again? _____

_____

CATCHING THE VISION

Watching and Discussing the DVD

Host Dr. Greg Smalley says ineffective communication is one of the greatest problems facing couples today.

To the rescue come Drs. Les and Leslie Parrott, popular authors and speakers on all things marital. Instead of telling us to talk, they show us how. In this video segment, they share two principles that can help every couple stay connected: clarifying content and reflecting feelings.

It's not enough to keep the lines of communication open; we have to make sure our messages are getting through. It's much more efficient than trying to repair the damage when we've been misunderstood.

After viewing the DVD, use questions like these to help you think through what you saw and heard.

1. Would being good at the following make you a good communicator in marriage? Why or why not?
   - debating
   - motivational speaking
   - sports announcing
   - newscasting
   - auctioneering
   - preaching

2. If you could read your spouse's mind, would your marriage be better off? Why or why not?

3. Drs. Les and Leslie Parrott say that a failure to communicate is the number-one complaint in marriages today. Do you think that would have been true in Old Testament times? New Testament times? The Middle Ages? Fifty years ago? Why?

4. Do you think most people feel better understood at home, at work, or at church? Is that because they tend to communicate more effectively in one setting than another? Explain.

5. Who's the best listener you've ever known? Did you like being around him or her? Why? What do think was that person's secret?

6. In the story about changing clothes, what went wrong with the Parrotts' communication? What could they have done differently to clarify content?

7. The Parrotts challenge the idea that women are better than men at reflecting feelings. Which of the following best echoes your reaction to that?
   - "Finally, somebody admits women aren't perfect."

- "When it comes to feelings, men really are tone-deaf."
- "So maybe I *can* communicate, even though I'm a guy."
- "Let's face it: We all stink at this."
- other _____

8. The Parrotts say it isn't enough to master the skills of clarifying content and reflecting feelings; you need to genuinely want to understand and connect with your spouse. Do you agree? Why or why not? How could someone who has only the skills also develop the right attitude?

Bible Study

An anxious heart weighs a man down, but a kind word cheers him up. . . .
A gentle answer turns away wrath, but a harsh word stirs up anger. . . .
Pleasant words are a honeycomb, sweet to the soul and healing to the bones. . . .
A word aptly spoken is like apples of gold in settings of silver.
(Proverbs 12:25; 15:1; 16:24; 25:11)

1. When you see in these verses that your communication should be kind, gentle, pleasant, and appropriate, what's your reaction?
   - "That's obvious."
   - "I can't be that nice all the time."
   - "Easy to say, hard to do."
   - other _____

2. When was the last time you did the following? What was the result?
   - tried to cheer up your spouse with a kind word

- chose to phrase a criticism of your spouse gently, not harshly
- kept your conversation upbeat for your spouse's sake
- considered before speaking whether it was the right time and place to say something to your spouse

A wife of noble character who can find? She is worth far more than rubies. . . .

She speaks with wisdom, and faithful instruction is on her tongue. . . .

Her children arise and call her blessed; her husband also, and he praises her. (Proverbs 31:10, 26, 28)

3. How do the wife, husband, and children in this passage communicate with each other?

4. How many minutes a day do you typically spend on each of the following? How do you feel about that?
   - speaking with wisdom
   - giving faithful instruction
   - calling your spouse "blessed"
   - praising your spouse

But I tell you that men will have to give account on the day of judgment for every careless word they have spoken. For by your words you will be acquitted, and by your words you will be condemned. (Matthew 12:36-37)

5. When you consider how you and your spouse have communicated since your wedding day, how do you feel about this verse? Why?

But the fruit of the Spirit is love, joy, peace, patience, kindness, goodness, faithfulness, gentleness and self-control. Against such things there is no law. Those who belong to Christ Jesus have crucified the sinful nature with its passions and desires. Since we live by the Spirit, let us keep in step with the Spirit. Let us not become conceited, provoking and envying each other. (Galatians 5:22-26)

6. What would you say to your spouse in the following situations, in a way that reflects the "fruit" listed in each case? How would you make sure your spouse understood the attitude you were trying to convey?

   - It's your birthday, and your spouse forgot [love].
   - Your child has been born with an operable heart defect [joy].
   - You and your spouse just left your freshman son or daughter at college [peace].
   - You're hanging wallpaper together, and your spouse can't seem to get it straight [patience].
   - Your spouse wants to sing in the choir, but can't carry a tune [kindness].
   - Your spouse is flirting with the idea of cheating "just a little" on your taxes [goodness].
   - You're addicted to Internet porn [faithfulness].
   - Your spouse is wearing plaid shorts and a striped shirt [gentleness].
   - Your spouse accidentally dropped your car keys through a sewer grate [self-control].

MAKING IT WORK

Applying the Principles

Try the following "mind-reading" game with your spouse.

In the box that follows, write what you had for a recent meal when your spouse wasn't present. Don't let your spouse see what you've written.

[empty box]

Now write your comments about a current film or song that you haven't discussed with your spouse yet. Again, don't let your spouse see what you've written.

[empty box]

Finally, write three numbers, three colors, and three first names. Keep these a secret for now, too.

[empty box]

Now stare at the first box while your spouse tries to "read your mind." See whether he or she can guess what you had at that meal. Then try the same with what your spouse wrote.

Do likewise with the other two boxes. Finally, discuss the results. How did the two of you do as "mind readers"?

Not very well, probably. So why do so many people fail to "clarify and reflect," expecting their mates to read their minds?

If possible, agree that next time one of you is bothered by the other's action, he or she will call a "clarify and reflect" meeting instead of relying on mental telepathy.

BRINGING IT HOME

Encouragement from a Counselor

Remember Caleb and Trina, who couldn't seem to find time to talk? They were referred to a marriage counselor. The first thing they learned was the "24-5 Principle"—based in part on Deuteronomy 24:5: "If a man has recently married, he must not be sent to war or have any other duty laid on him. For one year he is to be free to stay at home and bring happiness to the wife he has married."

If you're a newlywed, you can apply the 24-5 Principle by doing the following:

- Establish a special, exclusive covenant for one year.
- Refrain from all extra responsibilities during that year.
- Focus on and establish your marriage before you move out into career advancement, ministry, and further education.
- Invest in and bond with your spouse emotionally, spiritually, relationally, and sexually.
- Bring happiness to one another; limit your time with others during the first year.

You can expect some resistance from family members and friends on this decision. But ask them to pray for your marriage throughout this first year together.

What if you're past the one-year mark? You can apply the 24-5 Principle at any time in your marriage. Here are five steps to doing just that.

1. *Keep your promise.* Many couples, at their weddings, light a "unity candle" and blow out their individual candles. That symbolizes husband and wife dying to themselves in order to give birth to something new and much more intimate, beautiful, and mysterious—"two becoming one." One of the best ways to become one is to spend time together, and that can happen when you and your spouse talk, celebrate special occasions, set goals, go shopping, pay bills, play tennis, or study a devotional book.

2. *Be intentional and selective.* Everyone has the same amount of time—24 hours a day. Avoid being sloppy with yours.

Manufacturing more time isn't possible, but you can make excellent use of what you have by allocating time to talk and do things together. When that time comes, make sure you're rested and not rushed or preoccupied. If talking really is a priority for you, you'll say no to time-stealers like sitcoms, reality shows, and the Internet.

3. *Be creative and perseverant.* Talk about a variety of subjects—solving problems, overcoming challenges, establishing goals and priorities, your spiritual life, preferences, and just having fun.

4. *Enjoy and encourage uniqueness.* You and your spouse aren't alike. Think of how awful and boring it would be to be married to yourself! Those conversations wouldn't be very interesting, would they?

5. *Be loving, respectful, and patient.* The gift God has given you and your spouse is each other. Taking time to talk is part of that.

—James Groesbeck
Licensed Marriage and Family Therapist[4]
with Amy Swierczek

Chapter 3

LET'S TALK (PART 2)

Let's face it: Some topics are trickier than others. Even in the happiest marriages, issues like in-laws, finances, and sex can quickly shake things up.

Corey and Jen are building their first house. Every time Corey shares an idea about changes to the plan, Jen gets angry. Even when he tries to apologize, she may still attack him.

Corey knows that Jen has a difficult relationship with her father, a contractor in another state. Corey wonders if this influences her reactions to him, but doesn't know how to bring it up without making her mad.

When tough topics come up, couples can find lots of places to veer into the ditch. Many mistakes come from inexperience as husbands and wives bounce from one conflict to the next, experimenting with various solutions.

When it comes to talking about sensitive topics, some pitfalls are dug way before marriage. If you didn't get the right skills in your family of origin, it's hard to manage conflict with a spouse. The twin ditches of (1) avoiding conflict at any cost and (2) escalating into chaos are often more familiar than the path itself.

In addition to the old habits you bring into a marriage, new challenges can quickly crop up. Even the idyllic honeymoon phase can raise a number of touchy topics. A major purchase or holiday tradition can seem bigger than your relationship if you aren't prepared.

—Rob Jackson
Licensed Professional Counselor[5]

FINDING YOURSELF

Identifying Your Needs

Here's a survey to help you figure out how you're handling communication in your marriage.

1. How would you bring up the following subjects with your spouse?
   Where and when would you try to discuss them? Why?
   ____ whether to change the way your retirement account is invested
   ____ the fact that you just totaled the car
   ____ your dream of going back to school and getting a degree
   ____ biopsy results saying that you have cancer
   ____ your spouse's irritating habit of saying, "like, you know"
   ____ your desire to go to a marriage counselor

2. Which of the following questions do you think your spouse could answer about you? Does that tell you anything about how the two of you communicate? If so, what?
   ____ What was the most traumatic event of your childhood?
   ____ When did you first feel like a grownup?
   ____ Do you think the world would be better off without cell phones?
   ____ What was your biggest fear on your wedding day?
   ____ What would you miss most if your home burned down?

3. If you could change two things about the way you and your spouse tend to communicate, what would they be?
   ____ frequency
   ____ volume
   ____ topics

_____ attitude

_____ listening

_____ other _____

4. What's the most hopeful thing you've heard about communication so far in this course? _____

_____

5. What's one question you still have about communicating in marriage? _____

_____

6. Have you and your spouse discussed what you've heard in this group? Why or why not? _____

_____

CATCHING THE VISION

Watching and Discussing the DVD

What shuts down talk in a marriage? Sometimes it's a safety problem. One or both spouses feel a conversation is too risky—so they skip it.

In this DVD segment, Drs. Les and Leslie Parrott reveal four things couples need in order to feel safe enough to communicate—and how to get them.

Next, author and speaker Gary Smalley explains the deepening levels of communication couples can experience as they feel safer with each other. And don't miss Gary's surprising model for effective marital discussions: the fast-food drive-thru!

After viewing the DVD, use questions like these to help you think through what you saw and heard.

1. When you were growing up, did you ever dread having a conversation with any of the following? Why?
   - a teacher
   - a school principal
   - a parent
   - God

2. Drs. Les and Leslie Parrott describe a special room in which you and your spouse would always have great conversations. Try to imagine that room. What would it look like? What would make it feel "safe"? How much time would you want to spend in it each week?

3. The Parrotts point out that, in order to feel communicating is safe, some of us need to know that our time limits will be respected. If this is true of Husband A, which of the following do you think his wife should do to assure him that his time is protected when she wants to talk?
   - setting a time limit on the conversation
   - planning conversations in advance
   - saying, "My time is worth as much as yours"
   - starting the conversation just as he's drifting off to sleep
   - other _____

4. The Parrotts also note that many of us need approval in order to feel communicating is safe. How could your spouse let you know it's okay to bring up a sensitive subject, and that his or her love won't be withdrawn?

5. According to the Parrotts, some of us need loyalty to our established patterns in order to feel communicating is safe. Which of the following patterns are most important to you? Have you told your spouse about these? If not, would you like to?

- not raising our voices
- not interrupting favorite TV shows to talk
- not having serious conversations while driving
- not starting a conversation before or after a certain time of day
- not talking about personal topics in a restaurant
- other _____

6. The Parrotts observe that quality communication feels safest to some of us. How long would you want to discuss each of the following before you could make a "high-quality" decision? If possible, explain your answers to your spouse.
   - what kind of pizza to order
   - what kind of house to buy
   - what kind of treatment to get for cancer
   - what kind of clothes to wear to church

7. Gary Smalley describes six levels of communication in marriage, from superficial to intimate. Which of the following levels did you and your spouse reach in the last 24 hours? What kept you from reaching the "next level"?
   - clichés
   - facts
   - opinions
   - feelings
   - needs
   - beliefs

8. Gary suggests using the fast-food drive-thru as a communication model—asking a series of questions to find out what your spouse thinks, feels, and believes. What three questions would you ask in each of the following situations?

- Your wife comes home from work, shuts herself in the bedroom, and won't come out.
- Your husband admits that he's lost nearly $1,500 in online gambling.
- Your wife asks, "Does this dress make me look fat?"
- Your husband announces that he doesn't want to go to church anymore.

DIGGING DEEPER

Bible Study

A time to tear and a time to mend, a time to be silent and a time to speak. (Ecclesiastes 3:7)

1. Which of the following do you think are times to be silent? Which are times to speak? Why?
   - You're not sure what to say to your spouse, who is grieving the loss of a family member.
   - You're so angry at your spouse that your face is red.
   - Your spouse has embarrassed you in front of friends, and you think the silent treatment would teach him or her a lesson.
   - Your spouse doesn't seem to understand your sexual needs, and you're in no mood to explain them.

Instead, speaking the truth in love, we will in all things grow up into him who is the Head, that is, Christ. . . . Therefore each of you must put off falsehood and speak truthfully to his neighbor, for we are all members of one body. . . . Do not let any unwholesome talk come out of your mouths, but only what is helpful for building others up according to their needs, that it may benefit those who listen. (Ephesians 4:15, 25, 29)

2. When it comes to communicating with your spouse, is it harder to speak the truth, speak in love, or speak the truth in love? Why?

3. Rank the following kinds of "unwholesome talk" (in order from most to least) to show how big a problem you think they are in most marriages today.
   ___ profanity
   ___ gossip
   ___ sexual jokes
   ___ verbal abuse

4. If you had to "build up" your spouse with just two words, what would they be?

> *If anyone considers himself religious and yet does not keep a tight rein on his tongue, he deceives himself and his religion is worthless. . . .*
>
> *Speak and act as those who are going to be judged by the law that gives freedom, because judgment without mercy will be shown to anyone who has not been merciful. Mercy triumphs over judgment! . . .*
>
> *When we put bits into the mouths of horses to make them obey us, we can turn the whole animal. Or take ships as an example. Although they are so large and are driven by strong winds, they are steered by a very small rudder wherever the pilot wants to go. Likewise the tongue is a small part of the body, but it makes great boasts. Consider what a great forest is set on fire by a small spark. The tongue also is a fire, a world of evil among the parts of the body. It corrupts the whole person, sets the whole course of his life on fire, and is itself set on fire by hell.*
>
> *All kinds of animals, birds, reptiles and creatures of the sea are being tamed and have been tamed by man, but no man can tame the tongue. It is a restless evil, full of deadly poison.*
>
> *With the tongue we praise our Lord and Father, and with it we curse men, who have been made in God's likeness. Out of the same*

mouth come praise and cursing. My brothers, this should not be. Can both fresh water and salt water flow from the same spring? My brothers, can a fig tree bear olives, or a grapevine bear figs? Neither can a salt spring produce fresh water. . . .

Brothers, do not slander one another. Anyone who speaks against his brother or judges him speaks against the law and judges it. When you judge the law, you are not keeping it, but sitting in judgment on it. There is only one Lawgiver and Judge, the one who is able to save and destroy. But you—who are you to judge your neighbor?

Now listen, you who say, "Today or tomorrow we will go to this or that city, spend a year there, carry on business and make money." Why, you do not even know what will happen tomorrow. What is your life? You are a mist that appears for a little while and then vanishes. Instead, you ought to say, "If it is the Lord's will, we will live and do this or that." As it is, you boast and brag. All such boasting is evil. . . .

Above all, my brothers, do not swear—not by heaven or by earth or by anything else. Let your "Yes" be yes, and your "No," no, or you will be condemned. (James 1:26; 2:12-13; 3:3-12; 4:11-16; 5:12)

5. What percentage of marriages do you think are "set on fire" by words that could have been avoided?

6. What happens when the same person who sometimes whispers "sweet nothings" to a spouse is sarcastic and hurtful at other times?

7. What's something a spouse might say that exemplifies each of the following?
   - judging
   - bragging
   - not letting your "Yes" be yes and your "No" be no

8. If you were a counselor, how would you get couples to remember the principles in this passage?

MAKING IT WORK

Applying the Principles

Take a look at the following word balloons. Each contains a statement or question on one of the levels of communication Gary Smalley described on the DVD. Under each statement or question, write whether you think it's a cliché, fact, opinion, feeling, need, or belief.

Now choose one of the following topics:
- whether your spouse should get an annual physical exam
- what to do about clutter in your home
- whether the two of you are growing spiritually these days

Fill in each of the following blank balloons with a cliché, fact, opinion, feeling, need, or belief about the subject you chose.

Draw a star next to the balloon that represents the deepest level of communication you're currently comfortable with on that subject. If possible, talk with your spouse about where he or she drew a star. Take a moment to discuss what might help you reach the "next level."

Here's another communication exercise you can try this week. Declare a

room in your home the "drive-thru." The rule: In this room, you'll ask
your spouse, "May I help you?" at least once a day—and listen carefully
to the response. At the end of the week, discuss the following:

- Did asking "May I help you?" lead to any conversations or
  actions? Why or why not?
- Was it hard or easy to follow the rule?
- What other rule might make that room even safer for open
  communication?
- Would you like to try the experiment for another week? Why
  or why not?

BRINGING IT HOME

Encouragement from a Counselor

How can you prepare yourself to talk about sticky subjects? Here are three
suggestions.

1. Get practical skills. At the nearest Christian bookstore, you can find
strategies for dealing with sensitive issues. Shelves of books on marriage
address the role of communication. Improving body language, word
choice, and tone of voice will greatly improve your results.

So will picking a better time and place for your discussion. After
Corey and Jen made yet another frantic attempt to make decisions about
the new house amid piles of laundry and the cries of their baby, they
changed their approach.

"Look, Hon," Corey said. "We're never going to accomplish anything
like this. Let's get away and just talk over a nice dinner tomorrow night
when I get off work. What do you say?"

"If we can leave this discussion until then, I think I can handle it
just fine," Jen answered. "I'll call a sitter if you'll just promise me I won't
have to hear the words 'floor plan' or 'crown molding' until then. I'm

sure we can work something out if we calm down and put our heads together."

If you're trying to talk about a sensitive issue, get rid of distractions like television. Find a time free of interruptions. Still, don't let things get worse while you wait for the "perfect" time. It may never come.

One of the most practical things to do is to start your discussion with prayer. This habit can transform your marriage as you invite the Holy Spirit to guide your conversation. It also helps you steer clear of the pothole of confronting your spouse impulsively.

Speaking of steering, remember that driving along a cliff is even harder going in reverse. In other words, don't bring up past issues while trying to resolve new ones. If many of your old conflicts lack closure, get a mediator—a pastor or Christian counselor—to help bring your marriage up to speed and moving forward again.

2. Be principle-centered. Don't ask *who's* right. Ask *what's* right. Imagine a couple fighting over the perennially thorny issue of money. If both spouses take time to examine biblical principles of money management, they'll often emerge with a plan they agree on. The idea of attacking the problem, not the person, creates safety for sharing at a deep, effective level on any topic.

3. Partner with your spouse. While it's critical to find the truth about issues affecting your marriage, relationship is always more important than issues. You're partners, not prosecutors.

That partnership doesn't end when you discuss sensitive topics. Ask yourself whether you're showing your husband or wife the same respect you show your coworkers and friends. If you're Christians, ask yourself whether you're acting first as brother and sister in Christ, and second as husband and wife.

If the prospect of discussing a sensitive subject has you fearing (or worse yet, predicting) your spouse's reaction, you're losing focus. Your agenda should be to please God. If that's your goal, you won't hesitate to confront an issue like infidelity or addiction that tears your spouse away from Him.

That's what Elena did with Jacob. She'd debated for weeks whether to mention Jacob's new habit—playing online video games late into the night. She told herself that there were worse things he could do. But as a recovering bulimic, she knew firsthand that any compulsive behavior would eventually tear him down and damage their relationship.

Finally she decided to confront him: "Sweetheart, I know video games aren't immoral. But I'd like our day to end together." It was a first step toward a healthier relationship.

Talking about sensitive issues isn't easy, but it can make your marriage the vehicle that drives both of you closer to God. And two people with the same destination can't help but move closer to each other, too.

—Rob Jackson
Licensed Professional Counselor[6]

Chapter 4

SAFELY NAVIGATING THROUGH CONFLICTS (PART 1)

After only two years of marriage, Nancy and John are living very separate lives.

The problem? Neither of them likes conflict, so they avoid each other.

Nancy pours herself into hobbies and caring for their nine-month-old son. John is staying later at work, and often goes straight from there to the health club. On those nights he doesn't even see Nancy or his son before they go to bed. Using the excuse that he doesn't want to disturb his wife, he sleeps on the couch.

John and Nancy can't remember when they last had a night out together. Their sexual intimacy has dwindled to less than twice a month, with little tenderness or joy. Both are concerned about their marriage, but feel immobilized by the fear of getting angry, getting hurt, or hurting each other.

Maybe you can identify with Nancy and John. Unresolved conflict is hanging over your marriage like a thundercloud, threatening a storm you don't want to brave. Perhaps you've always resisted discussing problems. Or your efforts to resolve differences have ended in icy silence or shouting matches, experiences you don't care to repeat.

Not resolving conflict may give an initial feeling of peace or harmony, but it's like a wound that heals on the surface when underneath there's an infection that needs to be released. No one enjoys lancing the wound, but real recovery can't take place otherwise.

—Romie Hurley
Licensed Professional Counselor[7]

FINDING YOURSELF

Identifying Your Needs

Here are some questions to help you explore how you and your spouse
tend to handle conflict.

1. If a reality TV show followed you and your spouse around for a
   week, how would you want to change your usual way of dealing with
   disagreements?
   ___ stop throwing plates
   ___ hide the guns
   ___ speak more quietly and calmly
   ___ bring conflicts into the open
   ___ pretend you agree about everything
   ___ other _____

2. Which of the following sounds most like the family you grew up in?
   Which sounds most like your spouse's family? Why?
   ___ *World of Warcraft*
   ___ *Peace Like a River*
   ___ *The Negotiator*
   ___ *Fight Club*
   ___ *Silent Hill*
   ___ other _____

3. Which of the following do you think a couple needs to resolve in
   order to stay happily married? Why?
   ___ where to go to church
   ___ whether to spank the kids
   ___ how much money to spend on clothes

___ how often to call the in-laws

___ how often to have sex

___ who takes out the garbage

4. What's one thing you and your spouse have "agreed to disagree" about? How has that worked out? _____

_____

5. When do you think a couple should see a marriage counselor about conflict? Why? _____

_____

6. Do you think most couples are better or worse at handling conflict than you and your spouse are? Why? _____

_____

CATCHING THE VISION

Watching and Discussing the DVD

What's the number-one predictor of divorce? According to many marriage experts, it's the failure to deal with conflict.

Since couples can't help but clash sometimes, learning what to do about it is a number-one priority. In this DVD segment Dr. Gary and Barb Rosberg and Gary Smalley have fresh advice on how to face friction: Initiate forgiveness, treat your spouse as a best friend, be a "safe" person, and stop trying to change your mate.

Host Dr. Greg Smalley adds a personal story and wraps up with more tools for conflict-resolving couples.

After viewing the DVD, use questions like these to help you think through what you saw and heard.

1. If you've ever experienced the following, how did you feel at the time? What did you do about it? Why?
   - overheard a husband and wife arguing
   - seen spouses or partners physically fighting or throwing things
   - said something to your spouse that you regretted later
   - given or received the "silent treatment" for more than an hour
   - tried to mediate a conflict in another couple's relationship

2. Dr. Gary Rosberg says that failing to resolve conflict is the number-one predictor of divorce. Why isn't conflict itself the problem? Do you think most couples would rather have frequent, brief "blowups" or lingering, unresolved disagreements? Why?

3. Barb Rosberg says that every conflict contains something of value—including relational intimacy for spouses who work things out. What might a couple get out of resolving the following conflicts?
   - The husband wants to buy a boat; the wife wants to spend that money on a missions trip.
   - The husband wants to go back to college; the wife is tired of working.
   - The wife wants to adopt a child; the husband is afraid he'll fail as a father.
   - The wife wants to vacation in Las Vegas "for the sunshine"; the husband thinks it's wrong to support a "gambling town."

4. Barb suggests showing your spouse the same respect and restraint you'd show your best friend. If you treated your best friend the way you usually treat your spouse in the following situations, what would happen to your friendship?
   - Due to a misunderstanding, your friend shows up 45 minutes late for dinner.
   - Your friend leaves a pair of boots on your front step; you trip over them and skin your knee.

- Your friend forgets your middle name.
- At a party, your friend keeps blurting out the punch lines of jokes you're trying to tell.

5. Barb recommends using "I statements" when you're angry with your spouse. How could you turn the following "you statements" into "I statements"?
   - "You never stand up for me when your dad calls me a loser."
   - "You always make me feel like a heretic if I want to talk about changing churches."
   - "You've managed to ruin another perfectly good day."

6. Gary Smalley says that if we're "safe" people, our spouses will be drawn to us. Unsafe people, he adds, are judgmental, critical, angry, and trying to change others. Do you think your spouse would feel free to tell you whether you have any of those traits? Why or why not?

7. Gary says "safe" people are loving, kind, gentle, forgiving, tender, and compassionate. If a representative of the Marital Safety and Health Administration had observed your household last week, what letter grade might he or she give you in each of those areas?

8. Gary tells the story of how he gave up trying to change his wife. What part of the story do you relate to most? If you've been trying to change your spouse, how would it feel to accept him or her instead? Why?

DIGGING DEEPER

Bible Study

What causes fights and quarrels among you? Don't they come from your desires that battle within you? You want something but don't get it.

You kill and covet, but you cannot have what you want. You quarrel and fight. You do not have, because you do not ask God. When you ask, you do not receive, because you ask with wrong motives, that you may spend what you get on your pleasures. (James 4:1-3)

1. Which of the following unmet "wants" do you think lead to conflict in marriage? How?

    ____ love

    ____ sex

    ____ power

    ____ respect

    ____ other _____

    According to this passage, what might help?

    Do not envy a violent man or choose any of his ways. For the LORD detests a perverse man but takes the upright into his confidence. (Proverbs 3:31-32)

2. Based on this passage, how do you think God views physical abuse in a marriage?

    Hatred stirs up dissension, but love covers over all wrongs. . . . He who covers over an offense promotes love, but whoever repeats the matter separates close friends. (Proverbs 10:12; 17:9)

3. Does "covering over" wrongs and offenses mean sweeping them under the rug? If not, what does it mean?

    A man of knowledge uses words with restraint, and a man of understanding is even-tempered. (Proverbs 17:27)

4. How can you tell when you aren't using words with restraint? What kind of signal could your spouse give you when you're "crossing the line" during a heated discussion? What could you do to cool off?

> *Better a meal of vegetables where there is love than a fattened calf with hatred. . . . Better a dry crust with peace and quiet than a house full of feasting, with strife. (Proverbs 15:17; 17:1)*

5. Which kind of home described in these verses comes closest to the one you grew up in? How has that helped to shape the marriage you're in today?

> *Starting a quarrel is like breaching a dam; so drop the matter before a dispute breaks out. . . . He who loves a quarrel loves sin; he who builds a high gate invites destruction. (Proverbs 17:14, 19)*

6. Do you think some couples really "enjoy a good fight"? Why or why not?

7. In a marriage, where do you draw the line between matters that should be dropped and those that must be dealt with?

> *He who answers before listening—that is his folly and his shame. (Proverbs 18:13)*

8. If couples took this proverb to heart, what percentage of arguments do you think could be avoided? What percentage of arguments might become conversations? What percentage of conversations might be more productive?

Applying the Principles

Here are some road signs. How might the message of each sign apply to resolving conflicts between you and your spouse? Take a few minutes to talk about that. For example, "Stop Here on Red" could remind you to take a break during a heated discussion when you see your mate's face turning an angry crimson.

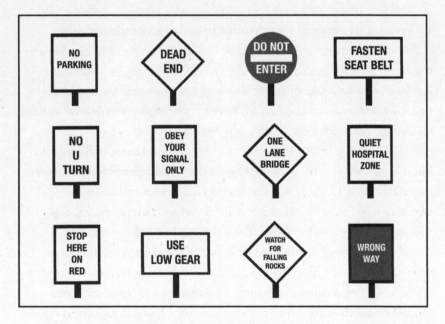

When it comes to handling conflict, which "rules of the road" are the two of you doing best on?

Which might you be "ticketed" on?

How can you go to "traffic school" when it comes to resolving conflict?

This week, consider Barb Rosberg's suggestion: praying after you and your spouse have discussed a conflict. What good might that do? What if you also prayed *before* the discussion? If you talk about a conflict this week, try either—or both—and see what happens.

BRINGING IT HOME

Encouragement from a Counselor

Fear of conflict can stem from having experienced too much of it as a child—or from never having seen any. Some parents shelter their children too much by not revealing disagreements nor demonstrating how they can be resolved. Others display only the arguments, not showing the process whereby disagreements are worked out, leading to a fear of the unknown.

In the case of John and Nancy, it would be good to share their childhood experiences with conflict and what their expectations were for marriage. They may discover that their expectations were unrealistic or mistaken—for example, thinking that Christians must never argue or disagree.

How couples deal with conflict is one of the greatest predictors of whether or not a marriage will end in divorce. In most marriages, conflict resolution is initiated by the partner who's more assertive or more of a pursuer physically and verbally. That can at least bring situations to the table, but the healthiest scenario requires freedom for both spouses to start conversations on areas of concern.

When both partners aren't assertive, or fear conflict, or lack the skills to deal with it, resentment can build quickly from the proverbial molehill into a mountain. It's crucial to get outside help in that case; you're dealing not only with personality issues, but most likely a lifelong pattern of avoidance. A good family therapist, or a pastor who has time and expertise to work with you on an ongoing basis, could coach you.

When unresolved conflicts are immobilizing your marriage, your goal should be to "get unstuck." Here are five steps in that direction.

1. Forgive your spouse.

2. Pray together.

3. Appreciate each other in a tangible way (cards, gifts, special meals, etc.).

4. Discover and confess stubbornness and the desire to be "right."

5. Get help from a wise mentor or counselor.

In the case of Nancy and John, it took a crisis to get them to a therapist. Nancy grew severely depressed and ended up in the hospital. John's concern for her, along with her doctor's prescription, drove them to see a Christian counselor.

After working with the therapist for several months, Nancy and John are less afraid of conflict. They know there's still a long road ahead, but are encouraged by how honestly they're expressing their feelings—especially when they remember how carefully they used to avoid that.

In addition, Nancy has been working out at the health club with John twice a week—while their son stays with John's parents. They go out to eat on those nights, and find they have energy and excitement for intimacy—and staying up later than usual.

—Romie Hurley
Licensed Professional Counselor[8]

Chapter 5

SAFELY NAVIGATING THROUGH CONFLICTS (PART 2)

You already know how you and your spouse deal with disagreements. Maybe you tend to knock a conflict over the head and bury it alive, hoping you'll never have to confront it again. Or maybe you let loose with verbal volleys that have plenty of volume.

Perhaps you've wondered, though, how your conflict management style compares to that of other couples. Since most husbands and wives avoid blowups in public, it can be hard to tell. Compared to them, are you normal? Average? Do they know something you don't?

Ben and Lisa are wondering that. As they look around the silent art gallery they're visiting, they don't notice any other couples who ooze hostility. Their own marriage, on the other hand, seems awfully turbulent. They argue often about how and where to spend their time and money. Lisa feels Ben's friends are always stealing him away. Ben thinks Lisa spends too much time on the phone, talking with her mother—and probably complaining about him. They've begun to withdraw from each other; when they do talk, their conversations usually end in a sarcastic verbal brawl.

Observing others' marriages, good and bad, may help you learn ways of resolving conflicts yourself. But the goal isn't to compare, compete, evaluate, or judge. It's to figure out what works best for you.

—James Groesbeck
Licensed Marriage and Family Therapist[9]
with Amy Swierczek

FINDING YOURSELF

Identifying Your Needs

To discover how you're dealing with some of the issues to be raised in this session, fill out the following survey.

1. Which of the following topics would you hesitate to bring up if you wanted to "keep the peace" in your home? Why?
   ___ politics
   ___ your spouse's appearance
   ___ your spouse's spending
   ___ your in-laws
   ___ sex
   ___ opinions about church or the Bible
   ___ other _____

2. Where would you go to feel safe in the following situations? Why?
   ___ an earthquake
   ___ a tornado
   ___ your home burns down
   ___ your spouse starts hitting you
   ___ you need to confront your spouse about a drinking problem
   ___ other _____

3. Which of the following rules do you and your spouse tend to follow when facing a conflict? Are you satisfied with the results?
   ___ If you can't say anything nice, don't say anything at all.
   ___ Don't bring up the past.
   ___ Listen twice as much as you talk.
   ___ Look for a win-win solution.

___ Make sure you understand what the other person means.

___ Don't say, "You always . . ." or "You never . . ."

4. If you could hire a full-time counselor to referee disagreements in your home, would you do it? Why or why not? _____

_____

5. Does the phrase "conflict resolution" describe what usually happens when you and your spouse disagree? Why or why not? _____

_____

6. Is it better for couples to fight, argue, debate, clash, seethe, explode, quarrel, squabble, or bicker? Why? _____

_____

CATCHING THE VISION

Watching and Discussing the DVD

What kind of atmosphere prevents conflict and promotes healing? Host Dr. Greg Smalley has an answer in this DVD segment, based on the findings of marriage researcher Dr. John Gottman.

First, couples need to accent the positive—because it takes five positive experiences to counteract one negative one. That's five compliments to every criticism. In fact, simply listing each other's positive traits can change spouses' attitudes in as little as a week.

Dr. Juli Slattery shares the rest of Gottman's prescription: Avoid criticism, contempt, defensiveness, and stonewalling, and develop a real friendship with your mate.

After viewing the DVD, use questions like these to help you think through what you saw and heard.

1. Can you name at least two positive things about each of the following? If not, why not? Why might some spouses have a hard time thinking of anything good to say about each other?
   - leaky fountain pens
   - asparagus
   - toxic waste

2. What's one of the nicest things your spouse has ever said about you? Is it easier to remember such compliments, or to recall critical things your spouse has said?

3. Dr. Greg Smalley says we need five positive experiences to counteract one negative one. What's your response to that statement?
   - "Life doesn't work that way."
   - "People shouldn't be so sensitive."
   - "I'm not sure I can provide that many positive experiences."
   - "Does pie count as a positive experience?"
   - other _____

4. Have a two-minute contest with your spouse to see who can list the most positive things about the other. Then, starting with the winner, explain whether this exercise had any effect on how you feel about your mate at this moment.

5. According to Greg, which of the following should a wife do if she's lost respect for her husband? Does this apply to husbands who've lost respect for their wives? Why or why not?
   - check her expectations to make sure they're realistic
   - work on her own beliefs, not her spouse's
   - focus on her husband's strengths
   - stop trying to control her husband
   - catch him doing things she respects

6. If the "Four Horsemen" of the marital apocalypse are criticism, contempt, defensiveness, and stonewalling, what might be the "Three Musketeers" of marital longevity?

7. Have you or your spouse ever used a "repair attempt," humor, or a catch phrase to halt an escalating conflict? Did it work? How do you know?

8. Spouses who hold each other in contempt are more interested in putting each other down than in solving problems. How might that approach seem useful for each of the following? Why doesn't it work in a marriage?
   - a talk radio host
   - a movie critic
   - a comedian
   - a professional wrestler
   - a candidate for public office

Bible Study

A man's wisdom gives him patience; it is to his glory to overlook an offense. . . . It is to a man's honor to avoid strife, but every fool is quick to quarrel. (Proverbs 19:11; 20:3)

1. Does our society offer more "glory and honor" for overlooking offenses and avoiding strife—or for "standing up for your rights"? What effect might this have on marriages?

Make plans by seeking advice; if you wage war, obtain guidance. (Proverbs 20:18)

2. How is resolving a marital conflict like "waging war"? How is it different? What kind of guidance should you get before entering this "battle"?

> Do not say, "I'll pay you back for this wrong!" Wait for the LORD, and he will deliver you. (Proverbs 20:22)

3. Do you tend to "pay back" your spouse for a perceived wrong by giving him or her the silent treatment, name-calling, taking "an eye for an eye," or in some other way? What would be a better course of action?

> Better to live on a corner of the roof than share a house with a quarrelsome wife. (Proverbs 21:9)

4. Are these the only two options? If not, what are some others?

> He who guards his mouth and his tongue keeps himself from calamity. . . . Through patience a ruler can be persuaded, and a gentle tongue can break a bone. (Proverbs 21:23; 25:15)

5. Why is it hardest to choose your words carefully when you're in the middle of an argument? What can you do next time you find yourself ready to go out of control verbally with your spouse?

> Do not answer a fool according to his folly, or you will be like him yourself. (Proverbs 26:4)

6. How do you tend to respond when your spouse says something you consider "stupid"? What might be a better strategy?

> A gift given in secret soothes anger, and a bribe concealed in the cloak pacifies great wrath. (Proverbs 21:14)

7. Do you think this proverb applies to conflict in a marriage? Why or why not? How does it compare with your efforts to "make up" after a disagreement with your spouse?

Applying the Principles

Seeing your spouse in a positive light and giving him or her positive reinforcement is one of the most important things you can do for your relationship. Take a few minutes to do that by creating some acknowledgments of your mate's qualities. Write on the following items as if you were giving them to your spouse. Be sure to show him or her the results. (Examples: "Master of Encouragement" diploma; "GoodKisser" blimp.)

As this session noted, many couples have used time-outs and catch phrases when they've felt overwhelmed during a conflict. Pick one of the following phrases to use this week if and when an argument gets over-heated. Then decide how long your time-outs will be if you need some.

- "Remember, I'm on your team."
- "I need some fresh air."
- "Is that an ice-cream truck I hear?"
- other _____

Encouragement from a Counselor

How do other couples handle conflict? In different ways, naturally. Some choose, after discussion, to set aside minor issues (how to put bowls in the dishwasher, as opposed to where to worship); others don't. Some couples consistently raise their voices—definitely not helpful.

Conflicts in marriage are common; unfortunately, handling conflict well isn't. But if you were to watch those who've learned how to resolve their differences, you'd see them taking some steps worth following. Here are eight of those steps.

1. *Face the facts.* All marriages—even healthy, vibrant ones—experience disagreements over issues like finances, jealousy, extended family, friends, sex, faith, and priorities. You and your spouse are imperfect; even at your best, you'll make mistakes. So it's important to develop a system of conflict resolution that fits your personalities and communication styles. Accept the fact that you'll face conflict—and commit to dealing with it.

2. *Take a time-out.* Rather than avoiding conversation or withdrawing altogether, take time-outs when things get dicey. When you're not making progress by talking, when you feel emotionally exhausted, or when the conversation becomes negative, step back and take a break. Time-outs can help you get a new perspective. Agree to continue the discussion constructively or end it until you and your spouse can handle it well.

3. *Watch your words and gestures.* Don't let your statements become destructively intense and disrespectful. Control your tone of voice and facial responses. No whining, shouting, pouting, sulking, sarcasm, or blaming. Don't give "the look" or roll your eyes.

4. *Value each other.* No matter what the difference of opinion may be, see your spouse as precious. Eliminate disrespectful behavior and

emotional put-downs. Choose to remove all name-calling, blaming, accusing, threatening, and manipulative speech from your conversation. Recognize that God has made every person unique and of eternal value.

5. *Think positive.* Choose to think the best about your spouse. When you find yourself consistently interpreting what your spouse says or does in a negative light, you're thinking the worst. Changing this can be a tough mental discipline that takes effort to establish.

To help you in this process, use the "Stop/Think/Decide" model. First, count to 10. Then identify the negative thought and question its validity. Replace it with a positive, accurate thought or belief—and say that to yourself and perhaps to your partner.

6. *Be a team.* Resolve to work together. Remember that you're on the same team with the same goal. Attack the problem, not each other.

7. *Listen intently and intentionally.* Take time to thoroughly talk and carefully listen to and understand each other. Distinguish between "relationship connecting" and "conflict confronting"; connect with each other before you confront problems.

Start by discussing only how you feel about the conflict; don't try to resolve it until both of you believe you've been clearly heard. Solving problems before connecting can cut off good discussion—temporarily reducing conflict but not truly resolving it.

8. *Keep getting together.* Establish weekly meeting times to deal with conflicts—and just to be with each other romantically and playfully. Plan "fun times" with no discussion of problems. Use those occasions to affirm each other.

No matter how other couples may handle conflict, you and your spouse are unique. Your Creator is the master artist, and the two of you are among His masterpieces. Keep learning about and enjoying your individuality, and you'll find it easier to deal with the differences.

—James Groesbeck
Licensed Marriage and Family Therapist[10]
with Amy Swierczek

Chapter 6

LANGUAGES OF LOVE

Monica sits in the counselor's office in tears. Ralph, her husband of three years, sits stony-faced, two feet away on the same couch, his arms crossed over his chest. The atmosphere is thick with her fury and his defiance.

She begins the session with a litany of Ralph's alleged failures, the worst being his neglect of her needs. He is, she says, "never home." Self-employed, he works long hours and takes frequent business trips.

When he's home, she says, he's either restoring an antique car or wanting to jump into bed for a quick sexual romp—for which he seems to have plenty of energy. When she's dead tired and turns him down, he pouts and sometimes storms out to the garage and his beloved Chevy. She notes with undisguised sarcasm that he's always too tired to just talk to her.

The final straw: Last week, on her birthday, he was gone on another business trip. She feels abandoned and unloved.

When Ralph finally speaks up, it's to say that things are usually much more peaceful in the garage than in the bedroom. At least the Chevy doesn't treat him like he's some dirty old man.

He can't understand why Monica is so angry about his long hours at work. She seems to him to have no concept of what it takes to earn the money needed each month to pay the bills. This is how a husband and father takes care of—loves—his family.

Of course he loves her, he says. Look at everything he does to be a good husband.

Standing outside looking in, it seems easy to see that when it comes to understanding each other's languages, Monica and Ralph are missing each other by a mile. In many respects, they exemplify stereotypical struggles with differences in communication.

—Phillip J. Swihart
Clinical Psychologist[11]

FINDING YOURSELF

Identifying Your Needs

How could knowing more about "love languages" help you? This survey may answer that question.

1. Which of the following would say "I love you" most clearly to your spouse? How do you know?

___ hearing you say "I love you"

___ spending an afternoon together at his or her favorite museum, park, hardware store, or mall

___ a gift of flowers, chocolates, or new computer software

___ changing a flat tire on his or her car in the rain

___ a massage

___ other _____

2. If your parents' marriage was relatively healthy, how did they tend to express love to each other?

___ by giving each other presents

___ with hugs and kisses

___ by cooking meals and mowing the lawn

___ through love notes and pet names

___ by spending time together

___ other _____

3. What kind of birthday card would your spouse like best?

___ one that pokes fun at the recipient's age

___ one with cats or dogs on it

___ a romantic one

___ a risqué one

___ any card, as long as it's funny

___ one with a serious poem

___ other _____

4. On a scale of 1 to 10 (10 highest), how well does your spouse seem to understand which expressions of love mean the most to you?

_____

5. Have you ever received a gift from your spouse that seemed totally unsuited to you? What did you do? _____

_____

6. Have you ever given a gift to your spouse that seemed totally unappreciated? How did you feel about that? _____

_____

CATCHING THE VISION

Watching and Discussing the DVD

Does your spouse really know that you love him or her? How can you "prove" your love?

Dr. Gary Chapman, author of the bestselling *The Five Love Languages*, explains in this DVD segment that there are five ways to express and perceive love: words of affirmation, quality time, gifts, acts of service, and physical touch. Your mate probably prefers one of these "love languages" over the rest. Gary shows how to "speak" that one, instead of sticking with *your* preferences.

Dr. John Trent wraps up this DVD with encouragement to start with little improvements in your marriage—the kind that are relatively easy and make a big difference.

After viewing the DVD, use questions like these to help you think through what you saw and heard.

1. Which of the following would mean the most to you? Which would mean the most to your spouse? What does that tell you about your respective love languages?
   • a surprise gift
   • hearing that your spouse is proud of you
   • spending a fall afternoon looking at the changing leaves
   • your spouse's decision to vacuum the floor or wash the car for you
   • a massage from your spouse

2. Which of the following sounds like something you'd do? Which sounds like something your spouse would do? What does that tell you about your respective love languages?
   • giving 20 kinds of perfume or cologne on your 20th anniversary
   • buying an "I love you" ad in the paper on Valentine's Day
   • going to two dozen garage sales together in one morning
   • changing the furnace filter because your spouse has allergies
   • holding hands all the way through a three-hour movie

3. Which of the following sounds like a complaint you might make? Which sounds like a complaint from your spouse? What does that tell you about your respective love languages?

- "All you gave me for my birthday was a toaster."
- "You never say you love me."
- "You're always at work or out with your friends."
- "You say you'll load the dishwasher, but you never do."
- "We never kiss anymore."

4. Which of the following sounds like something you might ask for? Which sounds like a request your spouse might make? What does that tell you about your respective love languages?
   - a new cell phone
   - your spouse's opinion of a poem you just wrote
   - to go out for coffee and talk
   - that your spouse would call the auto mechanic so that you don't have to
   - a hug

5. If someone had explained the "love language" idea to you when you were eight years old and asked you which language you liked best, what do you think your answer would have been? How did you want your parents to express love to you? How did you express it to them?

6. If Dr. Gary Chapman watched you and your spouse interact for a week, what do you think he'd say about your love languages? If he said, "You haven't given me enough information to go on," would that concern you? Why or why not?

7. What would you like to explain to your spouse about your love language? If possible, do that right now.

8. What did you think of the couple who decided to "start over" with love languages after decades of estrangement? Why were they willing to try? What can you learn from that story?

Bible Study

> *How beautiful you are, my darling!*
> *Oh, how beautiful!*
> *Your eyes are doves.*
> *How handsome you are, my lover!*
> *Oh, how charming!*
> *And our bed is verdant. (Song of Songs 1:15-16)*

1. What's the main "love language" demonstrated in this passage? What might be a modern equivalent of what's said or done in these verses?

    ___ words of affirmation

    ___ quality time

    ___ gifts

    ___ acts of service

    ___ physical touch

> *Come, my lover, let us go to the countryside, let us spend the night in the villages.*
>
> *Let us go early to the vineyards to see if the vines have budded, if their blossoms have opened, and if the pomegranates are in bloom—there I will give you my love. (Song of Songs 7:11-12)*

2. What's the main "love language" demonstrated in this passage? What might be a modern equivalent of what's said or done in these verses?

    ___ words of affirmation

    ___ quality time

    ___ gifts

    ___ acts of service

    ___ physical touch

We will make you earrings of gold, studded with silver. . . .

The mandrakes send out their fragrance, and at our door is every delicacy, both new and old, that I have stored up for you, my lover. (Song of Songs 1:11; 7:13)

3. What's the main "love language" demonstrated in this passage? What might be a modern equivalent of what's said or done in these verses?
    ___ words of affirmation
    ___ quality time
    ___ gifts
    ___ acts of service
    ___ physical touch

Strengthen me with raisins, refresh me with apples, for I am faint with love. (Song of Songs 2:5)

4. What's the main "love language" demonstrated in this passage? What might be a modern equivalent of what's said or done in these verses?
    ___ words of affirmation
    ___ quality time
    ___ gifts
    ___ acts of service
    ___ physical touch

Let him kiss me with the kisses of his mouth—for your love is more delightful than wine. . . .

His left arm is under my head, and his right arm embraces me. (Song of Songs 1:2, 2:6)

5. What's the main "love language" demonstrated in this passage? What might be a modern equivalent of what's said or done in these verses?
    ___ words of affirmation

___ quality time

___ gifts

___ acts of service

___ physical touch

MAKING IT WORK

Applying the Principles

Here are 10 expressions of love, based on the five love languages. Your job is to get specific. For instance, "Quality time that involves a can opener" might take the form of a gourmet dinner featuring various versions of Spam (if your spouse has a sense of humor).

Come up with the specifics for each expression of love. Then guess how your mate might react to each. Let your spouse confirm or contradict your guesses.

Based on your spouse's reactions, plan to express your love this week in a way that he or she will appreciate. Don't reveal your plan now, though; let it be a surprise.

1. Eight words of affirmation that do not include the word *love*

_____

2. Eight words of affirmation to the tune of "She'll Be Comin' 'Round the Mountain"

_____

3. Quality time that involves a can opener

_____

4. Quality time that doesn't involve food or drink

_____

5. A gift that costs less than $5

_____

6. A gift that's like one you gave your spouse a long time ago

_____

7. An act of service that requires wearing gloves

_____

8. An act of service that starts with the letter *d*

_____

9. Physical touch that leaves at least one person laughing

_____

10. Physical touch that would be rated "G"

_____

Here's something else to think about this week. Why do you suppose the DVD ended with Dr. John Trent's advice to make small improvements in your marriage? When it comes to love languages, what would be a "two-degree" course correction you and your spouse could make during the next six days?

BRINGING IT HOME

Encouragement from a Counselor

It's possible that the communication gap lies in how messages are perceived. But the style and content of the messages themselves differ, too. Men tend to use language to transmit information, report facts, fix problems, clarify status, and establish control. Women are more likely to view language as a means to greater intimacy, stronger or richer relationships, and fostering cooperation rather than competition.

In other words, it's "debate vs. relate." That means you and your spouse may be tuned into very different "meanings" in what each of you is saying. This provides fertile ground for misunderstanding, hurt feelings, and conflict. What one of you thinks is the other's "hidden meaning" can be 180 degrees out of phase with what the speaker really intends to communicate.

This can easily lead to distorted conclusions about the other person's motivations.

She's an unreasonable, demanding nag who won't leave me alone to watch the football game, he thinks.

He's an insensitive, domineering bore who doesn't have a clue about my feelings and doesn't want one, she tells herself.

Of course, one size never fits all. Females don't all fit neatly into one communication-style box and males into another. Some men can be quite nurturing and emotionally empathic in their language; some women are aggressive and task-oriented in theirs.

Still, you needn't be surprised if you and your spouse sometimes seem to need a translator. In his book *How Do You Say, "I Love You"?* (InterVarsity Press, 1997), Dr. Judson Swihart notes, "Often the wife comes in [to the marriage] speaking French and the husband speaking German—in an emotional sense. Unless you hear love expressed in a language that you can understand emotionally, it will have little value." The author goes on to say, "Fi uoy era gniog ot etacinummoc na edutitta fo evol drawot ruoy esuops, you must learn to speak his or her language."

It's hard to do that if, like too many couples, you enter marriage focused on being loved rather than on giving love. Try making it your goal not to change your spouse but to adapt to his or her style of communication. Turn your attention to hearing the heart of your partner rather than to the frustration you may feel about not being heard or understood.

If you feel stuck, and that your marriage is in a hole that just gets deeper, do something about it. Make a date with each other once a week to try a communication exercise. For example, the wife talks for 10 minutes about feelings or issues she has; the husband does nothing but listen. He may respond only with, "I don't understand; could you restate that?" or "What I hear you saying is . . ."

Then he talks for 10 minutes, and she listens. She can ask only for clarification or affirmation that she's hearing him accurately.

At the end of the exercise, neither of you is allowed to try to "straighten the other one out," react angrily to something you didn't want to hear, or debate the issue. During the next such "date," the husband will talk first and the wife second.

Other approaches to getting "unstuck" include attending a well-recommended weekend Christian marriage retreat, participating in a couples' support group through your church, or enlisting the help of a licensed Christian marriage counselor.

This is not a hopeless situation. In fact, compared to many marital conflicts, it's a state that can more quickly and remarkably improve—when two children of God who are committed to their marriage decide to work on it and seek appropriate help.

—Phillip J. Swihart
Clinical Psychologist[12]

NOTES

1. Adapted from Mitch Temple, "How Can I Adjust to My Spouse's Personality?" in *Complete Guide to the First Five Years of Marriage* (Carol Stream, Ill.: Focus on the Family/Tyndale House Publishers, 2006), p. 31.
2. Ibid, pp. 31-33.
3. Adapted from James Groesbeck with Amy Swierczek, "How Can We Make Time to Talk?" in *Complete Guide to the First Five Years of Marriage*, p. 206.
4. Ibid, pp. 206-208.
5. Adapted from Rob Jackson, "How Should We Talk About Sensitive Issues?" in *Complete Guide to the First Five Years of Marriage*, p. 212.
6. Ibid, pp. 212-215.
7. Adapted from Romie Hurley, "What If We Have a Lot of Unresolved Conflicts?" in *Complete Guide to the First Five Years of Marriage*, p. 258.
8. Ibid, pp. 258-259.
9. Adapted from James Groesbeck with Amy Swierczek, "How Do Other Couples Handle Conflict?" in *Complete Guide to the First Five Years of Marriage*, p. 229.
10. Ibid, pp. 229-232.
11. Adapted from Phillip J. Swihart, "Why Don't We Speak the Same Language?" in *Complete Guide to the First Five Years of Marriage*, pp. 199-200.
12. Ibid, pp. 199-201.

About Our DVD Presenters

Essentials of Marriage: Who Did You Really Marry?

Gary Smalley is one of the country's best-known authors and speakers on family relationships. He is the author or coauthor of 16 books that have sold more than five million copies combined, including *The Blessing* and *The Two Sides of Love*, which won the Gold Medallion award, and *The Language of Love*, which won the Angel Award. He has also created several popular films and videos. Gary has spent more than 30 years learning, teaching, and counseling and has spoken to over two million people in live conferences. He has appeared on national television programs such as *Oprah*, *Larry King Live*, and *Today*, as well as numerous national radio programs. Gary and his wife, Norma, have been married for 40 years and live in Branson, Missouri. They have three children, Kari, Greg, and Michael, and six grandchildren.

Dr. Gary Chapman is the author of the bestselling *The Five Love Languages* (more than four million copies sold) and *The Four Seasons of Marriage*. He is the director of Marriage and Family Life Consultants, Inc., an internationally known speaker, and the host of *A Love Language Minute*, a syndicated radio program heard on more than 100 stations across North America. He and his wife, Karolyn, live in North Carolina.

Dr. John Trent is president of the Center for Strong Families and StrongFamilies.com, an organization that trains leaders to launch and lead marriage and family programs in their churches and communities. John speaks at conferences across the country and has written or cowritten more than a dozen award-winning and bestselling books, including *The 2 Degree Difference* and the million-selling parenting classic *The Blessing* with Gary Smalley. His books, of which there are more than two million in print, have been translated into 11 languages. John has been a featured guest on radio and television programs including *Focus on the Family*, *The 700 Club*, and CNN's *Sonya Live in L.A.* John and his wife, Cindy, have been married for 28 years and have two daughters.

Dr. Gary and Barb Rosberg, cofounders of America's Family Coaches, host a nationally syndicated daily radio program and have conducted conferences on marriage and family relationships in more than 100 cities across the country. The Rosbergs have written more than a dozen prominent marriage and family resources, including *The 5 Love Needs of Men & Women* (a Gold Medallion finalist) and *Divorce-Proof Your Marriage* (a Gold Medallion winner). Gary earned his Ed.D. from Drake University and has been a marriage and family counselor for more than 25 years. Married more than 30 years, the Rosbergs live outside Des Moines, Iowa, and have two married daughters and four grandchildren.

Dr. Greg Smalley earned his doctorate in clinical psychology from Rosemead School of Psychology at Biola University. He also holds master's degrees in counseling psychology (Denver Seminary) and clinical psychology (Rosemead School of Psychology). Greg is president of Smalley Marriage Institute, a marriage and family ministry in Branson, Missouri, and serves as chairman of the board of the National Marriage Association. Greg has published more than 100 articles on parenting and relationship issues. He is the coauthor of *The DNA of Parent-Teen Relationships* (with his father, Gary Smalley) and *The Men's Relational Toolbox* (with his father and his brother, Michael). Greg, his wife, Erin, and their three children live in Branson, Missouri.

Dr. Les Parrott III is a professor of psychology and codirector with his wife, **Dr. Leslie Parrott**, of the Center for Relationship Development at Seattle Pacific University. He is a fellow in medical psychology at the University of Washington School of Medicine and an ordained minister in the Church of the Nazarene. Les earned his M.A. in theology and his Ph.D. in clinical psychology from Fuller Theological Seminary. Les has written more than 10 books, including *Questions Couples Ask, Becoming Soul Mates,* and *Saving Your Marriage Before It Starts* (all cowritten with Leslie).

Dr. Julianna Slattery is a family psychologist for Focus on the Family. Juli is the author of *Finding the Hero in Your Husband, Guilt-Free Motherhood,* and *Beyond the Masquerade.* Applying biblical wisdom to the everyday lives of women and families is her passion. She shares her message with a combination of humor, candor, and foundational truth. Juli earned a doctor of psychology and master of science in clinical psychology at Florida Institute of Technology, a master of arts in psychology from Biola University, and a bachelor of arts from Wheaton College. Juli and her husband, Mike, live in Colorado Springs and are the parents of three boys.

Mitch Temple is a licensed marriage and family therapist and author of *The Marriage Turnaround.* He holds two graduate degrees, in ministry and in marriage and family therapy, from Southern Christian University. Mitch currently serves as the director of the marriage department at Focus on the Family in Colorado Springs. He has conducted intensives nationwide for couples on the brink of divorce and has served as a family, pulpit, and counseling minister in churches for a total of 23 years. He was director of pastoral care, small groups, family ministry, and a counseling center at a large church for 13 years. He and his wife, Rhonda, have been married for more than 24 years and have three children.

FOCUS ON THE FAMILY®

Welcome to the Family

Whether you purchased this book, borrowed it, or received it as a gift, we're glad you're reading it. It's just one of the many helpful, encouraging, and biblically based resources produced by Focus on the Family® for people in all stages of life.

Focus began in 1977 with the vision of one man, Dr. James Dobson, a licensed psychologist and author of numerous best-selling books on marriage, parenting, and family. Alarmed by the societal, political, and economic pressures that were threatening the existence of the American family, Dr. Dobson founded Focus on the Family with one employee and a once-a-week radio broadcast aired on 36 stations.

Now an international organization reaching millions of people daily, Focus on the Family is dedicated to preserving values and strengthening and encouraging families through the life-changing message of Jesus Christ.

Focus on the Family
MAGAZINES

These faith-building, character-developing publications address the interests, issues, concerns, and challenges faced by every member of your family from preschool through the senior years.

For More
INFORMATION

ONLINE:
Log on to
FocusOnTheFamily.com
In Canada, log on to
FocusOnTheFamily.ca

PHONE:
Call toll-free:
800-A-FAMILY
(232-6459)
In Canada, call toll-free:
800-661-9800

FOCUS ON THE FAMILY® MAGAZINE	FOCUS ON THE FAMILY CLUBHOUSE JR.® Ages 4 to 8	FOCUS ON THE FAMILY CLUBHOUSE® Ages 8 to 12	FOCUS ON THE FAMILY CITIZEN® U.S. news issues

Rev. 12/08

More Great Resources
from Focus on the Family®

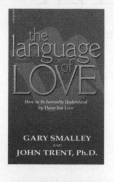

The Language of Love: How to Be Instantly Understood by Those You Love
by Gary Smalley and John Trent, Ph.D.
The frustration of missing out on meaningful communication affects not only our marriages but also our friendships, parent-child bonds, and professional relationships. Gary Smalley and John Trent deliver a time-tested method that enables us to bridge communication gaps, opening the door to greater intimacy and delivering lasting change! Paperback, includes study guide.

Complete Guide to the First Five Years of Marriage: Launching a Lifelong, Successful Relationship
Thousands of couples have asked the counselors at Focus on the Family for insight into money, communication, and a host of other issues. Now their collective wisdom is available for you in this handy reference book, the *Complete Guide to the First Five Years of Marriage*. Hardcover.

The Two Sides of Love
by Gary Smalley and John Trent, Ph.D.
Best-selling authors and family experts Gary Smalley and John Trent explain how to find a healthy balance between the protective, consistent "hardside" love and the tender, understanding "softside" love. By examining the four basic personality types, you'll learn how to best demonstrate both sides of love in all your relationships—and experience wholehearted love! Paperback, includes study guide.

FOR MORE INFORMATION

Online:
Log on to FocusOnTheFamily.com
In Canada, log on to focusonthefamily.ca.

Phone:
Call toll free: 800-A-FAMILY
In Canada, call toll free: 800-661-9800.

BPZZXP1